Name

Memories and Comments

Name

Memories and Comments

Name

Memories and Comments

Memories and Comments

Name

Memories and Comments

Name

Memories and Comments

Name

Name

Memories and Comments

Name

Memories and Comments

Name

Memories and Comments

Memories and Comments

Name

Memories and Comments

Name

Memories and Comments

Name

Name

Memories and Comments

Name

Memories and Comments

Name

Memories and Comments

Memories and Comments

Name

Memories and Comments

Name

Memories and Comments

Name

Name

Memories and Comments

Name

Memories and Comments

Name

Memories and Comments

Memories and Comments

Name

Memories and Comments

Name

Memories and Comments

Name

Name

Memories and Comments

Name

Memories and Comments

Name

Memories and Comments

Memories and Comments

Name

Memories and Comments

Name

Memories and Comments

Name

Name

Memories and Comments

Name

Memories and Comments

Name

Memories and Comments

Memories and Comments

Name

Memories and Comments

Name

Memories and Comments

Name

Name

Memories and Comments

Name

Memories and Comments

Name

Memories and Comments

Memories and Comments

Name

Memories and Comments

Name

Memories and Comments

Name

Name

Memories and Comments

Name

Memories and Comments

Name

Memories and Comments

Memories and Comments

Name

Memories and Comments

Name

Memories and Comments

Name

Name

Name

Name

Memories and Comments

Memories and Comments

Memories and Comments

Memories and Comments

Name

Memories and Comments

Name

Memories and Comments

Name

Name

Memories and Comments

Name

Memories and Comments

Name

Memories and Comments

Memories and Comments

Name

Memories and Comments

Name

Memories and Comments

Name

Name

Memories and Comments

Name

Memories and Comments

Name

Memories and Comments

Memories and Comments

Name

Memories and Comments

Name

Memories and Comments

Name

Name

Name

Name

Memories and Comments

Memories and Comments

Memories and Comments

Memories and Comments

Name

Memories and Comments

Name

Memories and Comments

Name

Name

Memories and Comments

Name

Memories and Comments

Name

Memories and Comments

Memories and Comments

Name

Memories and Comments

Name

Memories and Comments

Name

Name

Name

Name

Memories and Comments

Memories and Comments

Memories and Comments

Memories and Comments

Name

Memories and Comments

Name

Memories and Comments

Name

Name

Memories and Comments

Name

Memories and Comments

Name

Memories and Comments

Memories and Comments

Name

Memories and Comments

Name

Memories and Comments

Name

Name

Memories and Comments

Name

Memories and Comments

Name

Memories and Comments

Memories and Comments

Name

Memories and Comments

Name

Memories and Comments

Name

Name

Memories and Comments

Name

Memories and Comments

Name

Memories and Comments

Memories and Comments

Name

Memories and Comments

Name

Memories and Comments

Name

Name

Memories and Comments

Name

Memories and Comments

Name

Memories and Comments

Memories and Comments

Name

Memories and Comments

Name

Memories and Comments

Name

Name

Memories and Comments

Name

Memories and Comments

Name

Memories and Comments

Memories and Comments

Name

Memories and Comments

Name

Memories and Comments

Name

Name

Memories and Comments

Name

Memories and Comments

Name

Memories and Comments

Memories and Comments

Name

Memories and Comments

Name

Memories and Comments :

Name

Name

Memories and Comments

Name

Memories and Comments

Name

Memories and Comments

Memories and Comments

Name

Memories and Comments

Name

Memories and Comments

Name

Name

Memories and Comments

Name

Memories and Comments

Name

Memories and Comments

Memories and Comments

Name

Memories and Comments

Name

Memories and Comments

Name

Name

Name

Name

Memories and Comments

Memories and Comments

Memories and Comments

Memories and Comments

Name

Memories and Comments

Name

Memories and Comments

Name

Name

Memories and Comments

Name

Memories and Comments

Name

Memories and Comments

Memories and Comments

Name

Memories and Comments

Name

Memories and Comments

Name

Name

Memories and Comments

Name

Memories and Comments

Name

Memories and Comments

Name   Memories and Comments

Name   Memories and Comments

Name   Memories and Comments

Name

Memories and Comments

Name

Memories and Comments

Name

Memories and Comments

Name

Memories and Comments

Name

Memories and Comments

Name

Memories and Comments

Name   Memories and Comments

Name   Memories and Comments

Name   Memories and Comments

Name

Memories and Comments

Name

Memories and Comments

Name

Memories and Comments

Name

Memories and Comments

Name

Memories and Comments

Name

Memories and Comments

Name

Memories and Comments

Name

Memories and Comments

Name

Memories and Comments

Name   Memories and Comments

Name   Memories and Comments

Name   Memories and Comments

Name

Memories and Comments

Name

Memories and Comments

Name

Memories and Comments

Name   *Memories and Comments*

Name   *Memories and Comments*

Name   *Memories and Comments*

Name   Memories and Comments

Name   Memories and Comments

Name   Memories and Comments

Name   Memories and Comments

Name   Memories and Comments

Name   Memories and Comments

Name

Memories and Comments

Name

Memories and Comments

Name

Memories and Comments

Name

Memories and Comments

Name

Memories and Comments

Name

Memories and Comments

Name

Memories and Comments

Name

Memories and Comments

Name

Memories and Comments

Name

Memories and Comments

Name

Memories and Comments

Name

Memories and Comments

Name

Memories and Comments

Name

Memories and Comments

Name

Memories and Comments

Name

Memories and Comments

Name

Memories and Comments

Name

Memories and Comments

Name

Memories and Comments

Name

Memories and Comments

Name

Memories and Comments

Name

Memories and Comments

Name

Memories and Comments

Name

Memories and Comments

Printed in the USA
CPSIA information can be obtained
at www.ICGtesting.com
LVHW080738011023
759636LV00035B/17